How to Take Wildlife Photos with a S...

The Birds and the Bees

How I use My Smartphone to Capture Flying Animals

C. Mahoney

Life is about choices...

I walked toward the harbor's inlet, smartphone in hand, hoping to sneak up on a floating bird. I had the camera app already open and my fingers at the ready. As I neared the rocky ledge, I stepped quietly and slowly. One step, another, and there was a *great blue heron*. I raised my smartphone just as it lifted its wings and began to fly away from me. Click. One photo, and this is what I got. All I had was my Samsung Galaxy S-series phone. I didn't need anything else.

What do you notice about this photo of a *honeybee*? Did you notice how I chose a single flower, away from all the others? Did you notice that my camera blurred the background, allowing you to focus on the flower and honeybee? Did you notice that I used the sun's natural lighting (not my flash) to showcase the yellow petals of this daisy? Can you see the sun highlighting the honeybee's wings and hairy body? Yes, yes, yes and yes? Of course.

I don't like to waste time when I am out looking for birds (like this *American robin*) to photograph. So, I set my smartphone to open the Camera app when I double-press the home key. I don't actually have to look at my phone to do this. I do it by touch as my eyes are searching for movement. Open your camera, press the gear icon, and toggle the switch on for "Quick launch". Now you can be ready for that amazing photograph when it happens.

When I saw this *bumblebee*, I smiled. I like their fuzzy bodies and the claws at the end of their legs. I like seeing their translucent wings motionless, and then watching those wings pick them up from a flower and move them to another. If you look carefully, then you will see that both antennae are pointed down toward the flower to help it find what it is seeking. And its proboscis (the mouth part that contains its tongue) is uncurling right now. Amazing!

What do most people do with the photos they take at parties, restaurants, the mall or the hospital? They post them on Instagram or Facebook. We're all about documenting the memorable moments of our lives. That is what I do with my wildlife photos, like this one of a *great blue heron*. But I crop them first. You can do this by opening your Gallery, selecting a photo, pressing the crop box icon, dragging the edges to where you want them to be, press Save, and then Share.

The sun was directly overhead (around noon) when I walked outside and saw this *bumblebee* on the front porch. I pulled out my smartphone and took this photo. I did not need a flash to capture its shiny carapace or its black eyes or its hairy legs. So, when is a good time to go look for bugs, and does it matter if it is sunny or overcast, and should I go looking for bugs when they are still cold and still from a night of resting? Go anytime! Just go!

Video or photo? Since I create books (I have over a thousand at Amazon), I prefer photos. But, you can set your smartphone to record a short "Motion video" for each photo you take. Open your camera, press the gear icon, and toggle the switch on for "Motion photo". It will show you what the critter did the second or two before your camera took its photo. I turned off this feature on my phone, but you may like it and choose to keep it active. How about this female *mallard*?

Did you know that you can use your voice to take a photo? If you open the camera app, press on the gear icon, and toggle on the "Voice control," then you will be able to tell your camera to take a photo instead of pressing the LCD screen. Just say "capture" (or "cheese" or "shoot" or "smile"). This feature makes capturing insects more fun, I think. So, what do you think of this wasp? Are you afraid? Don't be. I've never been stung on a hunt for bugs.

Sometimes all you will get is a quick shot of something memorable. As I was kayaking on a nearby river (3 miles away), I saw a *hawk* high in the sky. I had my smartphone in a fanny pack (facing the front). I unzipped the pouch and pulled out my phone. When that hawk saw me, it came over to investigate. This photo shows it turning away at the last second (and let out a screech) when it realized that I was not food.

If you want to take a good photo, then take lots of them. No, don't stand in one place and keep taking the same photo of a gray and black striped *bee* again and again. Move around to change your angle and what is in the background. Get closer or farther away to include different stuff in your shot. Capture the left side of the insect, the right side, the head facing you, a top view. Variety, variety, variety. That is one of the major secrets of wildlife photography.

Why take photos of wildlife? Hmmm. Good question. Let me explain it in one sentence, a question. How does a bird fly? Look at this photo and you'll see how a *morning dove* moves from the edge of a hill and down through a valley. Look at how the feathers are spread out, and the angle of the wings, and how high they are above its head. Only a photo taken in real time, as a startled bird flies off toward safety, can answer that question about flight.

Pretty amazing details of this *bumblebee*, eh? Did you know that smartphone comes with a feature which allows you to review a photo as soon as you take it. You can take a photo and then look at it to determine if it is what you wanted. I turned off this feature on my phone so that I can quickly take wildlife photos in succession. If you want to turn it off, then open the camera app, press the gear icon, and toggle off the "Review pictures" option.

Sometimes my enthusiasm for wildlife overtakes my practical disposition. I really wanted a photo of this *robin*. Really! But the product became a mess as my camera fought against the absence of light (cloudy day) and the distance (up in a tree) and the myriad of branches in the way (what to focus on). When you see a bird in a tree, stop, empty your hands, and enjoy a minute of observation. Watch. Notice its behaviors. And smile.

Sometimes wind is a problem for a wildlife photographer. On days when there are gusts up to 15 m.p.h., I don't go looking for flowers or bugs. Why? Insects, like this *honeybee,* have trouble flying when the wind isn't cooperating, so they often don't. And getting a flower to stop moving so that your camera has the time to focus can be very frustrating.

Don't chase wildlife. That is a phrase I hear again and again from other wildlife photographers. Get what is within reach or within view. If you see a *great blue heron* fly away from you, don't chase it with the hope of getting that awesome shot. It already knows that you're near, and it is leaving the area because you make it nervous. Switch your focus to something else (or you will waste time and just get frustrated).

When I walked outside to let my dog use the restroom, I saw bees and wasps and flies of many types visiting the dandelions in my yard. So, I went back inside, grabbed my smartphone, and took some photo. In this photo of an iridescent *bee*, I captured it from above, so that I could have a bright yellow background for my subject. Sometimes I use a forty-five-degree angle, or a ninety-degree angle. That means getting low to the ground and sometimes lying on my belly.

I cropped this photo. Would you do it as I have? I wanted to include the fullness of this *bald cypress tree* to show where I stumbled (or kayaked) upon a pair of *mallards*. Yes, they are swimming away from me while keeping an eye (just one) on me in case they must fly to safety. Which duck is paddling the most right now? For the answer, look at the water being displaced in front of each duck.

The best time to find bees or *wasps* or butterflies is in the spring and summer when the sun is shining for longer periods of time each day and the flowers are responding accordingly. Insects and flowers have a symbiotic relationship. Each provides something for the other while taking what they need. If you want to photograph pollinators, then plant flowers outside your home. Or visit friends who have flowers and spend a few minutes outside taking photos.

When you think of birds, does your mind conjure up images of cardinals or blue jays? Or, if you live in a city, maybe you're thinking of wobbly pigeons and noisy crows. This *gray heron* is about three feet tall and has a wingspan of six feet. I saw it as I paddled in my kayak. My smartphone is easy to carry and doesn't demand lots of balancing and caution. Getting out in nature broadens my view of things, from the little to the big, from plain to colorful.

This insect is not a honeybee. It is a *hoverfly,* and it is harmless. My smartphone came with decent storage capacity, but I store all my photos on a micro SD card. You can do this by opening the camera app, pressing the gear icon, and selecting "SD card" under Phone storage. I do this so that if my phone's memory got wiped, then I wouldn't lose any of my wildlife photos.

As I look at this *seagull*, I can't help but wonder what it is doing. It may be looking for food. Or, it could be getting ready to go back to the location where it roosts at night. Or, it could be airing its wings for the sake of cleanliness. Or, it could be looking for another seagull to be with. Or, it could be passing time by riding the air currents. I don't know, but a photo makes me wonder what it is doing. That is what I often do, wonder.

This is exactly what I found and where I found it. I didn't move anything. Some *hawk* (I believe) lost a feather while in flight or in a fight, and this is where that single feather landed. So I must ask, is a hawk a hawk because of all that makes it a hawk (body, feathers, experiences, food inside its belly)? And is it less of a hawk once it loses a part of itself (like a feather)? I don't know, but images of birds or their feathers arrive with questions like this.

What do you think I was trying to photograph in this photo? the leaf? the plants in the distance? Of course not. I wanted the camera to focus on the black *wasp*, while also keeping the rest of the leaf in focus. To do this, I pressed the part of the LCD screen that showed the insect, and the camera followed my directions and focused the lens there (not the center of the screen which is the green leaf).

I felt at peace and calm while watching two *ducks* glide past me on a lake. I took their photo and brought it home so that I could remember this moment. I cropped it so that the ducks were as large as I could make them, while also including their reflections. I do this a lot, including a reflection or shadow in the photo I capture. Whether it is a tree's reflection on still waters or a bug's shadow on a leaf, I include both to give the viewer a more complete view of what I saw.

This is the underside of a leaf. A *firefly* or *lightning bug* was hiding there. As I walk along a trail, I often will stop at a tree and look up at the leaves. I find spiders, flies, beetles, and lots of other insects seeking shelter there. They do this to cool down (avoiding the direct sunlight), or to stay dry (avoiding the rain), or to hide from predators (avoiding death by bird). Be patient and thorough, and you'll occasionally be rewarded with a surprise like this.

My camera is always with me, even on a Sunday when I was arriving at my church (Unitarian Universalist). It is March, and *geese* spend mornings looking for something green and crunchy to eat. I didn't have to drive anywhere special for this photo. I just went were I frequently go, and I took advantage of the situation.

It is just a *feather*, right? Nothing important. Just a discarded part of some bird. Well, I love finding and photographing things in the water, objects that only recently fell into the water and have not become water-logged or mushy. You can still see the fine barbs and pointy edges. The depth of the water provides a dark background for this white feather. I like it. How about you?

There is a "rule of thirds" in photography. Imagine that there are two horizontal lines dividing this image into thirds (and vertical lines doing the same thing). Photographers try to place something along those lines instead of centering everything in the middle of the frame. Often, this comes during the post-production work when cropping an image. To see these lines, open the Camera app, press the gear icon, and select 3 x 3 under "Grid lines".

Your phone can track a moving insect (like this *bumblebee*) and make photography easier for you. Open the camera app, touch the gear icon, and toggle on "Tracking AF". AF = autofocus. I touched the image of this honeybee on my LCD screen and the camera stayed focused on this insect for the next few photos as it lifted off and tried to get away. Notice the details of its hairy abdomen, its clawed feet, and the nectar attached to its middle legs and antennae.

Every camera has a *depth of field* limitation. If you take a photo of something in the distance, then everything will appear in focus. No problem. But if you take a photo of something nearby, like this *long-jawed orb weaver* clinging to a branch, then everything too close or too far away will be blurry. Your smartphone cannot render everything in perfect clarity. It must choose what to focus on, and you must decide what that is.

When I saw this *tent caterpillar*, I didn't just take one photo and walk away. I took a shot from about three feet away and another from about two feet. I try photos that are directly over the bug as well as from the side angle of the bug to show its legs or length. And I take shots from the front to show its face, both head-one and diagonal. Variety is important when taking photos.

Sometimes you find something worth taking a photo of that is just "Wow!" When I saw this *feather* during a kayak ride, I pulled out my smartphone and coasted by (to keep the waves to a minimum). I had to avoid the sun reflecting off the water (it was off to the left), yet I used it to highlight the edge of the feather. Click! Got it! What you see is exactly what I saw. No touching. No rearranging. No contact at all.

What is this *blue jay* looking at? Can you see its head turned? Did it hear a friend, or a competitor? Is it worried about a hawk, or wanting to find food? If you shoot into a dark tree canopy, then you must tell your camera where to focus. I pressed the LCD screen where the blue jay was perched on a limb. My camera did its best to focus here, leaving nearer and more distant branches blurry. Still, the image is grainy and dark.

When I want to show a friend my wildlife photos, I open a folder I created called "Wildlife". To create your own folder, open the Gallery app, click on the three dots in the upper right-hand corner, select "Edit", choose the photos you want to place in a new folder, click on the three dots in the upper right-hand corner again, select "Copy to album", select "Create Album", name the album and then select "CREATE". Now you have a special album for your wildlife photos.

I encourage you to practice some of the steps that I use to capture wildlife. You can do this in your own yard, in a city park down the road or along the trail of any state/national park. The world is full of strange and beautiful creatures, so get out there and find them. Your body will feel better with the exercise, and your mind will enjoy the searching and discovering along the trails. So, what are you waiting for? Go outside!

This book is part of a series. Go to amazon and look for some of the other amazing books in my "How to Take Wildlife Photos with a Smartphone" series:

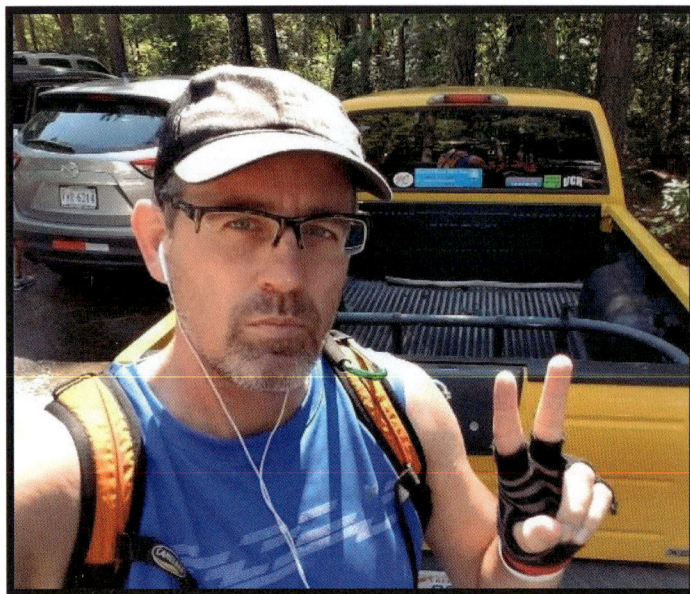

- ➢ Beetles and Bugs
- ➢ Bugs on Flowers
- ➢ Butterflies, Moths and Caterpillars
- ➢ Deer, Squirrels, Rabbits and Raccoons
- ➢ Dragonflies and Damselflies
- ➢ Getting Close to Spiders
- ➢ Grasshoppers, Katydids and Crickets
- ➢ Snakes, Turtles, Frogs and Lizards
- ➢ The Birds and the Bees
- ➢ Wandering Ants and Pesky Flies

Printed in Poland
by Amazon Fulfillment
Poland Sp. z o.o., Wrocław